Pebble Rings

Poems

by

Judy Ray

Some of these poems have appeared in the following publications: *Ambit* (London), *Assembling No. 7, Blue Unicorn, The Greenfield Review, Helicon Nine, The Kansas City Star, Lucille, Nimrod, Poetry Now, The Syracuse Review, Thicket* and *West Branch*.

Publication of this book has been made possible, in part, by small press grants from The New York State Council on the Arts and The National Endowment For the Arts.

ISBN # 0-912678-42-9
Library of Congress # 80-65816
Greenfield Review Chapbook # 42

Cover photograph by Judy Ray

Greenfield Review Press
Greenfield Center, New York 12833

for David,
for Sapphina,
for my mother,
and in memory of my father

CONTENTS

I. Searching for apple trees

On an Indian Miniature: "Girl Awaiting Her Lover"   9
The Nun On The Train   10
A Fire in Wales   11
For My Father   12
Asking Directions in York   13
The Pig Man of Yorkshire   14
For My Mother   15
Rose Bay Willow Herb   16
London Loneliness   18
The Night Light of Divorce   20
"What Child Is This?"   21
The Scythe   22
Written On My Father's 86th Birthday   23

II. A beach of stones

The Pebble Ring   27
Here and There   28
The Telephone   29
In Your Absence   30
The Belly Dance Class   31
"The Daily Round, The Common Task"   32
Child's View Of Mr. Nixon   33
Sex Education   34
An English Girl Dreaming In America   36
A Henry Moore Exhibition At The Tate Gallery   37
Lost Treasures   38
Herble The Hamster   40
An Easter Day   41
Villanelle: As You Seek Truth   42

III   Landmarks

Mexico, 1971   45
El Hospicio de Niños, Guadalajara   46
Indignant Pigs of Ajijic   48
Photographs of Mexico   50
A Dream   53
The Parcel   54
For Karl Wallenda, Tight-Rope Walker   55
Fire Temptation   56
Drinking in Africa   57
The Pigmy Mother at Bundebugi   58
Flamingoes   60
Beethoven   61
The Cemetery in January   62

I Searching for apple trees

On An Indian Miniature:
"Girl Awaiting Her Lover"

She is poised and proud,
    waiting under the starry tree;
her feet are turned away in delicacy,
    yet the look is bold.
She will dance for him,
speaking with graceful hands
    and armlet bells.
Will he learn the secrets
    beyond her art?
Or will she always be mysteriously
    hidden, though wrapped
        in transparent veils?

The Nun On The Train

Riding on the train
through summer banks of stitchwort
and forget-me-not
    forget-me-not
        forget-me-not
a nun nods in the heat.
She cannot loosen her heavy black dress
or tight white chinstrap
so her cheeks turn pink.
What does she think,
behind softly moving lips,
of those thighs of mini-skirted girls
flirting with the Italians across
the aisle? What does she think
of the woman glimpsed in a bikini
painting window frames?
                    And what
does she think of
Roderick Random in my lap,
and even of my new red shoes?

A Fire In Wales

No dragons today, I said.
Only light mist over the Brecon Beacons.
Please, no dragons today
in Newport, South Wales,
though they may fly above on the flags.

But here, right on the street
is a yellow one, tame, I see,
with a name—Snorkel, in high black letters.
Its long jointed arm holds up
observers crowded in a box,
excited as early balloon travellers,
flapping arms, pointing down.
They are inspecting the site of the
Corner Discount Store, where another
fiery dragon blazed. Gaping walls
still smoulder. Metal skeletons
with flesh and clothes burned away.
Wheels of sewing machines, twisted
sculptures, pots and pans, kettles
blacker than they'd ever be
from a roadman's brazier or a
hobo's open fire.

All drenched now. The Saint George
firemen are turning away from battle,
taking off their armour.
But wait. A hiss from the corner.
This dragon is not dead.
It hisses like the one in my head,
making me cross over mountains
to this grey town.

Dragons are hard to kill.

The mist has come down now over the Beacons.
Dense. Like smoke.

For My Father

Sturdy English oak, deep-rooted
in the Wealden clay,
now ivy is slowing down your pacing
still in muddy fields
to sow, mend hedges, count cattle
or grow an oasis of vegetables and roses
in a wilderness of stinging nettles.
You take pride in your honesty
yet know that acorns are the food of pigs.
The brown eyes, looking at England
for eighty-three years now
have dimmed, yellowed like the leaves
in autumn.
Through two World Wars, when brothers
and nephews wore uniforms,
and bombs left smooth craters even
in the quiet Front Meadow,
you went on supplying milk and sugarbeet.
But when an angry cow attacked,
you threw the toddling daughter down
beneath you in the ditch
and took the goring horn in your own back.

Asking Directions in York

A long journey, look-
ing for love or peace
at the confluence
of these slow rivers,
the Foss and the Ouse.
The search must go back,
it seems, through armies
of the white roses,
through mystery plays,
to twelfth century
towers of the mass-
ive minster, where aisles
and trancepts form the
cross. I must circle
ancient walls, past Good-
ramgate, Micklegate
and Skeldergate. The
longest name of the
shortest street carved in
flagstones where the girl
stands pointing: Turn right—
   W H I P M A W H O P M A G A T E .
Go down there as far
as ever you can
go. But you won't go
far, you won't go far.

The Pig Man of Yorkshire

In early morning I watch
the village wake. It isn't
"Under Milk Wood," but North Dalton
at the edge of the moor. I
have walked so far, narrow
road between high hawthorn hedges.
Now a blond boy is calling
in the heavy cows. He will
not stay. His eyes are looking
to new towns rising from the
ancient stones.

In the next field the pig man's
ritual begins. He is
a little man with bent legs;
the sack of feed lies across
his shoulders like a yoke. He
dances in a circle and
the feed spills as he tips and
jogs and jigs. The sows squeal and
snuffle up behind him. His
face is pink and grey as theirs;
he grins at me even now
across the shining water trough.

For My Mother

"But the child that is born on the Sabbath Day
Is blithe . . ."

You leaned against the kitchen post, weary
from summer cooking of ripe greengages
just hours before you lay back to greet me
wailing on the Sabbath that presages
blithe days, for youth, at least. Beside that black
oaken post you stooped to throw logs or coal
into the sooty iron stove, pushed back
fine golden hair, mixed cakes in earthen bowls.
And you were always there, weaving your way
around that room, that oak maypole adorned
with shine of hands and cracks, where hang today
bouquets of all the seasons—sharp blackthorn,
honesty, brown beech leaves, and mistletoe—
all woven with your two score years times two.

Rose Bay Willow Herb

The willow herb, the
rose bay willow herb,
sweeps woods and commons
with pink sunset stripes.
It rises from black
aftermath of fire
that crackled through thick
undergrowth of trees.
Even after war
it flourishes in
empty lots, in bomb
craters, and like a
phoenix of flora
rises tall and wild,
true fireweed, indeed.
Should the air it spikes,
water it drinks, ash
it grows from become
radioactive,
the invisible
aftermath of a
great folly, perhaps
the willow herb, the
rose bay willow herb,
will still grow wild with
pink sunset stripes and
bloom abundantly.
But who will there be
of our coughing, skin-
flaking, misshapen
kind to perceive a
symbol of hope? And
perhaps the only
phoenix to arise
from that blind folly

will be some tiny
flung molecule of
untainted earth with
no memory of
tall willow herb, wild
rose bay willow herb.

London Loneliness

This woman once loved and laughed.
Now she breakfasts on boiled eggs,
discussing Heinz factories
with Australians in the
crowded boarding house, and runs
down Earls Court Road in half light,
in sleet to the tube. Pushing
bodies, fur coats, spotty necks—
collage of nightmares. A green
eye bright with turquoise shadow
peers from a stout man's lapel;
his bulbous drunken nose is
a beetroot squeezed dry of juice.

From coughs and gloomy silence
she climbs above the lofty
Bank to lofty offices
to take dictation from a
cross-eyed woman soon to be
fuzzy in the head. The take-
home pay will take her home by
rush hour tube but not much more.

This city's romance can be
lost on one who feels the stones
a lonely prison, who tramps
by Brompton's cemetery
again and again to read
the large sign: NO THOROUGHFARE.
No indeed.
             Or should she choose
bright-lighted Piccadilly
with two million wanderers,
half a million of them drunk
on Saturday nights, or stay

at the boarding house and hear
bottles smashing in the road
to the old-time tune, "It's a
long way to Tipperary."

How long will this woman need
to get in out of the rain,
to pass by the graveyard gate
and keep on going down Old
Brompton Road into and beyond
the center, to somewhere she
can belong,
      to green oceans,
to the warm hands of someone
from another world.

The Night Light of Divorce

A slab of light strikes the ceiling
        of this room across from
        King's Cross Station,
railway lines
        leading past sodden backyards,
        where cabbages are yellowed
        and hopeless.

A slab of light—it should be me.
One corner with sharp lines,
        seven years shut off.
Another corner sparkles, an outward star,
        my child:
        I am afraid for this fragile beam.
Opposite the light is pure with love
        but I am dimmed.
And the last edge is rounded
        like the world
        leading into shadows from the guillotine
                                or courthouse pillars.

"What Child Is This?"

(for Sapphina)

The cloth was blue, shading into cloud-white.
I pinned the hem as the dream-child turned.
Each time she faced me the skirt was too short,
for between turns this child went spinning,
circling into giddiness, not yet knowing
how to whip the head around
like a dancer.
I knelt to reach.
She laughed, and cried, and went spinning
back over the river
still flowing under the ice,
to be teased by the snake roots
of bending trees.
Next time I grasped more firmly, safe
landing on the slippery bank.
Marking off inches on a ribbon
to measure a mother's face,
she tries to steady the dizziness.
We walk away.
The river twists itself before us many times
with its opposite leering bank,
faithless creepers, and rocky water.
We walk away.
Hand in hand, we walk away.

The Scythe

Curved wood, curved blade.
Rolling waves of land.
Grasp firmly the grained,
weathered handles,
and sense the ripple of muscles
swinging, stooping, swinging
in harvest sweat and dust.
The sweep of woody grain
becomes a path
that I am following towards
the old man with beard of mist
at edge of fields, edge of woods,
edge of the earth,
who stands in the path,
grey scythe against grey shoulder.

The path has not been
without rocks, gulleys, brambles.
I have passed through
a wall of swarming locusts,
a whirring, gossiping cloud in the desert.
I have crossed a living rope
of ants marching greedily.
I have faced a barrel,
escaped the flash
of blade on flesh.

Now in parting fog
the grey tangled thorn
fades but does not disappear,
bars the way
                though there is no way

Written On My Father's 86th Birthday

Dreaming, I see how it will be.
Two apple trees are missing.
The garden is dug and raked
smooth, ready now for planting.
Long rows are staked out
but the earth is waiting.
Where is my father? I ask.
Is he gone now, who bent
and hoed, whose wellington boots
kicked stones from this same earth
that is waiting? Dew falls
like tears, and blue mist
streaks the fields.
My mother doesn't answer.
She has become a moonbeam
leading into the darkness,
whispering to willows.
Nightingales are silent,
searching for apple trees.

II   A beach of stones

The Pebble Ring

(for David)

Seven years ago
you gave me a white pebble
from the ocean,
a ring that spoke
of the sea's swelling
and of our love.
I lost the ring in the cold
white of icy Alps.
Perhaps it was carried back
with melting glaciers
to a beach of stones,
where it goes on whispering
of love and of giving,
where new lovers will kneel.

Here and There

Do you like it
in this arched white house
On the wooden platform
above the cobbled koklakia floor?

Do you like it
in the bed and breakfast room
Blue on a seaside afternoon
looking for the farthest shore?

Do you like it stepping
from this Spanish sidestreet into a day hotel,
Burnished mirrors, bare room,
moving beyond all lies?

Do you like it in this lake
where the fish are dying,
The last people in the wilderness
reflected in our eyes?

The Telephone

Hullo? Hullo?
I can sell you
an air-conditioned
nightmare, and a
ticket to Katmandhu
to escape it.
I can send whispers
hissing in your ear,
put you on hold
with heavy breath, become
the song thrush
of your dreams.
And I can call, even
across ocean ice floes,
I love you,
I love you, I love you

In Your Absence

Tonight   your side of the bed
lies flat   in white moonlight
tall windows   Perhaps
you've climbed   the beanstalk
of streaming light   to become
the moon   changeable
mysterious   wise
My arm   across the deserted covers
where you are not
finds the light   cold

The Belly Dance Class

"I have walked through many mirrors
But always unaccompanied."
—John Peale Bishop

Shoulders are loose but there's no
shimmy in the thighs. Snaking
arms can undulate but the
knees won't bend.
How do they do
that cobra coil in the fourth
dimension?
Nobody has it
quite *all* together. Spirit
is willing, but zills clash out
of time.
Body rolls now,
thrusting forward and up,
arching back and down. Turn up
the insinuating slow
music. Now
watch the girl with
red rippling hair whose movements
are sinuous suddenly
and smooth, like an angular
giraffe rocking across the
wild plains.
A floating veil
becomes mist, a mantle of
light. She glides away to her
new rhythm, and vanishes
through the mirrored wall.

"The Daily Round,
The Common Task"

Their living room is heaped with dirty junk—
    dust, toys, clothes,
    broken shards of anger—
the trashy trimmings from twelve years
of marriage, all downhill.
She pushes her bottle behind the spider plant,
and watches him scrabble through the mess.
She has already given up
but he, this precise engineer
    of ambition
    and prejudice
is trying to find the limits,
and yelling: If I find still here
just six pieces of that broken glass
you threw at me last month, I will
    not
    take you out to dinner!

Child's View of Mr. Nixon

She wrote on the bathroom wall:
NIXN IS A DRTE PIG,
then did a jigsaw puzzle
of the Presidents with his
heavy jowled face at the top.
"Ooh, look at Richard Nixon.
I just don't know why Mrs.
Nixon would want to marry
him. I guess he failed school too.
And you don't even learn
everything you need to know
at school. I bet he failed school
25,000 years in a row."
Perhaps that is the way
history will count it, too.

Sex Education

She listens with big questioning
eyes as we read *How Life Begins*.
She's looking for the chapter on
"The Higher Forms of Life." And we've
already learned much back in "Birds"
and "Fish," poring over dancing,
courting gulls, and those compulsive
journeys of the salmon leaping
falls to reach fresh water pools of
birth and death.
But now we marvel more at the
instinct of eels. Along the
eastern shores of America
and western shores of Europe
they come to feel their one-time life-
consuming seven-year-itch. Then
they hurry in the waters of
autumn, nine hundred miles east or
four thousand miles west to the whirl-
pool of nowhere, the Sargasso
Sea. Three thousand feet down in the
inky cauldron they spawn and die.
Millions of new eels float up, and
by a miracle receive the
brand of citizenship, for those
spawned from eels of Europe head east,
and the others head west, slowly,
two or three years on their growing
trip. What confusion there would be
if the male eels made a mistake
and fertilized the wrong batch of
floating eggs. The new generation
wouldn't know which way to turn and
would have to swim forever round
the Sargasso Sea. These statements

of science are bewildering
still. How was the inside infor-
mation obtained? Some sex clinic
must have donned frog masks and wet suits
for an unbelievable chase
of tail led by an aquatic
Masters and Johnson.

An English Girl Dreaming
In America

A burst of syringa shines
in a dark garden where leaves
glisten with rain. The window
stretches tall as a palace
tower. A queenly lady
sparkling with jewels and a
ruff white as the syringa
looks out across the spires
and grey walls of a small town
over fields that sweep down to
the ocean. With steady gaze
she sends forth red sailing ships,
swooping gulls, and watches their
passage through a diminished
ocean to another coast,
a new England, or age-old
America. In one dream
glance the child encompasses
her history. She calls out
"There's the bush that snows," and wakes
to white syringa blooming
in an emerald garden.

A Henry Moore Exhibition
at the Tate Gallery

Past discs of moon-face and green-lined polish
of bronze, my slow, yes, sheep-like wandering
through the Birthday Exhibition leads me
to reclining figures, familiar holes
and hollows where it wouldn't be so hard
to fall right in.
                          A bearded, sensuous
artist from Germany, timing his walk
to my sheep-bell, tries to reason with me:
"It's in his drawings," he says, "that space leads
into objects. But here in full form the
objects are pushing outwards into space.
You don't feel that?" On the close crater's rim
I gasp, No, and the guard frowns.
                                        I grope from
the three-part figure towards a safer
"Upright Piece" in Rose Aurora Marble.
Such smoothness, Oh shining upward smoothness,
of this knifed torso with uneven arms,
a thin edge of perfect balance. I lean
closer to peer, as if it were a pool
for Narcissus, and seek the secret of
the balancing form on a compass point,
but reel back startled, struck by some outward
thrusting force. That smooth spire pushed me away?
I lean close again and sway off balance
backwards from the marble strength, expecting
to hear alarm bells ringing.
                                    The German
artist grins and offers coffee, but I
couldn't tell whether space held out the sides
of coffee cups or was itself contained.

Lost Treasures

(for Sapphina)

You hang the bountiful dowry
of necklaces from Mardi-Gras
around the tabby corner cat
whose eyes flash as he darts
beneath a spreading juniper,
climbs a walnut tree, then is free
of the treasure, glorious burden.
You run to search the bushes
—flashlights, torn shirts—
but nothing shines to light.
You yell at the cat, betrayed.

For comfort and distraction
I tell you of other treasure hunts.
Back on the farm, your uncle
had a special sport. In a small field
called Pug's Bottom, tucked away
in woods, rabbits would always hide
in the last triangular stand of wheat.
Driving the harvester around, your uncle
would keep one tense hand on the wheel.
He had a favourite spanner, and a quick eye.
He'd hurl that weapon from the
moving tractor and kill a rabbit outright
as it ran in panic.
Once he threw but in the stubble
could not find the tool again.
At every ploughing or harvest
of that field he thought of it.
He'd turn up Roman coins
in the heavy clay, or ancient ink-pots,
or bubbling bottles
with glass marbles still inside the necks.
But a full fifteen years went by

before that favourite spanner
clinked again to the surface.
Gleaning it from rough ground he knew
the rabbits, safe through all those years,
were laughing in the woods.

And on that same farm your grandmother
once lost her wedding ring
in high autumn grass.
In springtime a royal thistle
grew tall in the wild border,
wearing a crown, a gold band
above its purple robes.

So miracles do happen, you see.
Let's look again for your necklace,
    when the moon is full.

Herble The Hamster
1-1-79

Herble
wasn't a gerbil,
had no long tail to
swing from bars. But her
tiny hamster hands,
delicately pink,
begged against the white
soft belly hair when
she sat up looking
for the tidbit you'd
bring in your own quick
hands. You thought she
might be hibernating,
lying still in brown
oak leaves, but it was
the stillness of death
and she did not wake
into the New Year.
So you label a
tiny necklace box,
HERBLE: REST IN PEACE
and cover the eyes
that briefly shone like
jewels.

An Easter Day

Marigolds on window sills
Giving new life to old pans.
Children letting go the toad,
With blessings. Fra

Lippo Lippi frolicking
Through these leather-bound pages.
Then wild, wild wind and darkness
Of sudden storm.

From green sky glares a strange blood-
Red sun spelling Holocaust
In startled eyes, fire creeping
From clod to clod, up the hill
To roads that cross.

Villanelle: As You Seek Truth

As you seek truth in a chaos of lies
the city's clamour becomes desert where
you sift sand, winnow out all but the wise.

In the uniformity of franchise
wasteland, you are blinded by billboard glare
as you seek truth in a chaos of lies.

Since in sermons, statistics, slick advice,
one word of truth, one poem, might lie snared,
you sift sand, winnow out all but the wise.

Rainbow wigs, dreams sold for gain, a disguise
of time, of greed—disguise to be laid bare
as you seek truth in a chaos of lies.

From city masks you turn to dunes that rise
with shifting shapes, a wind-blown strand, and there
you sift sand, winnow out all but the wise.

This Herculean task you organize
into a harvest of gems, pure and rare.
As you seek truth in a chaos of lies
you sift sand, winnow out all but the wise.

III   Landmarks

Mexico, 1971

Above the town the road becomes
a rock-strewn path
where donkeys bring down basket loads
of firewood, and thorn hedges straggle
around tiny, cracked
mud houses.
Children peep and push
from dark doorways.
"Why do they have raggedy clothes?"
my daughter asks. "They wouldn't
want my T-shirt would they? All we have
to give them is balloons."
As we blow up the coloured fancies,
looking down on pink cathedral towers
where fire balloons float above
fiesta fireworks on New Year's Eve,
the children sidle up, stumbling
over chickens and a sleeping pig.
That moment of shy smiles
still haunts me, those ludicrous
ephemeral balloons hanging over
thorns and cactus points.

El Hospicio De Niños, Guadalajara

In the austere chapel of
the Hospicio de Niños the
flaming soul of Orozco
is flung on to walls like an
ocean raging against
a rocky island.
He painted the spirit of
revolution, machine men
harsh and hard, conquistadors
becoming their own
steely armour. He painted
sacrificial hearts, arrogant priests
and horses.

Outside, the columned courtyards
seem warm as a burro's back,
quiet as a hive of drones.
This is the dream of Bishop Cabañas,
the padding feet of orphans
on cobblestones.

From a corner doorway wafts
a swarm of infants,
the girls pink-smocked.
A tiny boy confronts you at your knee,
looks up, shading his eyes:
—Papa?
You blindly stare, also dazed and lost,
as you recognize your search in his.
—Papa? —No, little one, no.
Not here. Not there.
(How many strangers will he have to ask?
How many indifferent heads
will shake and turn away in the sun?)

What you must do, little one,
is find comfort in Orozco's
fiery men and chains,
and listen for the iron
hooves to come trampling down
from chapel walls.

Indignant Pigs of Ajijic

Market day. The bus is full.
But everyone must get on,
elbows drawn in, baskets gripped
tighter, the heat endured. And
underneath, in the dark 'hold'
of the busy bus, young pigs
are still squawking, together
with roosters and hens, legs tied,
thrust there for the slow jolting
journey of nightmares.

The siesta calm of an
afternoon is broken by
sharp squeals as four men drag one
heavy and indignant pig
down the street to the dusty
courtyard of his new owner.
The pig heaves himself against
a lamppost, refusing to
turn the corner, there where we
watched the villagers perform
a ritual drama at
the Christmas season, dressed in
satin and ribbons and robes,
dancing devils and singing
angels, bells on their tall staffs,
weighing up the confessions
of those who parade around
the drawn-up lines, as in a
country dance. Now it takes four
men with ropes and sticks to drag
this pig with relentless high-
pitched scratch of squeal along the
cobbles and gutter as he
splays resisting shiny feet.

At night in dim moonlighted
courtyard a huge sow lies on
her side, a mass of piglets
swarming against her so that
her body undulates like
a huge queen ant pulsating
from the centre of a mon-
umental ant hill. She lies
in mysterious shadows,
luminous complacency.
No indignation until
a feast day, or the early
hour of the rooster's call.

Photographs of Mexico

The ruin of a Mayan temple
bluntly points the island
where cliffs drop away
to the crashing Caribbean sea.
A Japanese traveller
whose silhouette breaks the wide sky
braces himself against rocks
to photograph the sun-baked hollows
of an ancient altar.
Then he hands down the camera
to his girlfriend, a lithe
and bikini-clad *gamin* from France,
and disappears over the steep cliff
with harpoon and diving mask.
When he climbs up, brown
and glistening, he carries a large fish,
holds it up for the camera click,
a tranquil scene of triumph
and survival.

To the north, in the fishing village
with idyllic palm-fringed
beaches of white sands,
the wind whips around corners,
boxes clatter clumsily down the street.
Sand rises, stings the face,
grits the mouth, as the wind's roar
grows louder than the constant waves.
Scurrying home with bent heads,
neighbours call out, "It's the norther,
the three-day norther."
The ferry boat is due tonight.
Crowded and waterlogged it ploughs
dizzily towards the dock where
the Japanese traveller

stands, his camera zooming in
on frightened faces of huddled
families crossing themselves,
clutching babies and bags, staggering
incredulously to the slippery
wet dock. He takes away pictures
of fear and flying spray,
of clicking beads and the hands
of a ferry boat captain
gripping a tiller.

The island is narrow and green,
a giant lizard in the sea.
From the village the road runs
like a crooked spine to bare rocks
of the sacred Mayan point.
Midway, between mangrove swamps,
a sputtering motorbike takes a corner
too fast. In sudden silence
wheels spin uselessly beside a young man
in the ditch, a deep hole in his forehead,
blood spurting. One jagged rock
stands out in all that green—
like a tombstone.
With wads of tissue and instinctive
action, murmuring "Lo siento, señor,
lo siento mucho" as pressure must go on
the wound to stop the spilling blood.
And waving down the road to find
a good samaritan on wheels,
pleading with drivers who don't want
any blood on their cars.
"It's a matter of life or death.
Please, señor." But death is always
around some corner, even though
Saint Christopher dangles from the mirror.
A red and battered pick-up truck coughs
to a stop. In the back stands

the Japanese traveller
with camera focused on the rock
of sacrifice, the victim.
His Panama hat is new and gleaming.
He does not move, except to wind on
his stilled pictures, taking in
all the green, and dust,
and splashes of red.

The earth shudders, moves cramped muscles.
It shakes again and the island splits.
The village crumbles.
The Japanese traveller
wears a red cross badge on his shirt,
dried fish tied at his belt.
He photographs the stretching chasms,
steps back as they grow,
steps back, and back, down the narrow
island to the cliff-top temple,
with widening lens to take in
all the sacrifices falling into
this greatest of all cenotes.
Pyramids topple, their secrets intact;
altars with dried blood, or rocks
sharp on a boy's temple; a motorbike
crumpled like a dead branch.
And the sea pounding through,
churning over bright fish and coral,
battered boats and coconut palms,
towards an open shutter.

A Dream

I am turning the handle
    of an old-fashioned mangle.
The clothes start pressing through.
But these are not just trousers, brown and corded;
they are legs, bent at the knee,
    twisted and lame.
This flattened T-shirt is the striped
round body of a child.
And a sheet drawing through so slowly
    is a shroud.
There is writing on all these "clothes,"
words printed from the mangle rollers.
    And faces too.
Not even faces, just expressions.
Dark patches of pain and anger,
a curled up corner for enticement
and flat calm for sleep.
    Wrinkles everywhere
on these grotesquely mangled bodies.
And I cannot lean back on the handle,
    cannot stop these rollers.

The Parcel

Always there is the parcel
that cannot be lost.
And always I must travel,
though I know this dusty road
is everywhere the same.
Sometimes the parcel is brown
and tied with string,
slipped into a basket.
If I leave the basket
in a crowded bus, hidden
behind a pineapple
it will, nevertheless, be on the train
almost covered
with an old tarpaulin.
The jewelled lady on the train
is a stranger, yet she knows me,
gives me a piece of silk
from her sari
with elephant embroidery.
Wrap your parcel in this, she says,
and give it to the beggar
at the temple.
The blind old man knows me, too,
feels my face, puts my parcel
beside his bowl.
His skin turns white
when he kisses me.
And he gives me presents to take away,
picking them up delicately
from market stalls. *A sweater*
for your man, he says. Silk scarves,
tiny china coffee cups. Caressing,
blessing each gift, he says again:
Take these. I will keep
your parcel.

For Karl Wallenda,
Tight-Rope Walker
22 March, 1978

Old man, were you afraid? Or
did you live so long with fear
balanced beside your thin steps
that it disappeared? Your show
became a metaphor, that
line we walk above shadows,
the tumbling out of order,
sons before fathers.
                    High winds
took you, trembling, from the wire.
But before you fell, old man,
I believe you really flew.

Fire Temptation

You are subtle, fire, starting out of sight
under weathered floorboards of this old porch,
smouldering till you blaze into a torch
that cries destruction to a street of white

wooden houses. When I see you caress
the peeling walls I'm drawn in close enough
to smell the crackle, feel the heat, see puffs
of wanton smoke. Now you move in careless

play, and I, who should be the town crier
of news, ringing loud bells, only advance
to where you leap like a Kikuyu, dance
like Shiva. My shining eyes take you, fire,

blazing to the next porch the next white wall.
But then I seem to see again haystacks
burning, flames creeping to a barn where sacks
of harvest grain were stored; before the fall

of ancient black beams of oak everything
was tried, the ground laid bare, the ponds pumped dry.
So—singed, and awakened at last from my
hypnotic trance, I jump back, run shouting

for hoses, for help, for water, to save
these quiet old houses from the glory
of ravaging fire, from the strange story
of one who danced, rejoiced—the fire-god's slave.

Drinking In Africa

Pombe is for the people,
brewed from green matoke;
fill the gourds at twilight—
a cousin has come from the country.

Don't trust the pineapple—
that *munanasi* is a wily serpent.
Just three days to be humming strong.
Then it turns, with a whiplash.

Pombe is for the people,
and for the wife-beating, as if
with great banana stems. Neighbour's shrieks
echoing down the valley. All is well!

Waragi, the moonshine of shadows,
is a devil that burns out brains
and eyes. The lees are left by the roadside,
red dust for a shroud.

But *pombe* is for the people,
sipping through thin reeds
from one huge gourd in firelight,
sharing tall tales on a green night.

The Pigmy Mother At Bundebugi

I think she really meant it,
but I've never been quite sure,
as I am not sure now that
I was ever there, behind
the Mountains of the Moon
above the Semliki
plains of elephant grass.

Our descent into a
jungle crowd of pigmies
was so sudden—perhaps the
one who danced into the road
with drawn bow was a mirage.
But out of trees, or nowhere,
families drew close, young boys
and girls already as tall
as their elders. Fiercely they
rushed to sell us their wares,
plunking on tiny lyres
homemade from gourds, shaking
hairy black and white skins
of colobus monkeys,
waving bows and arrows
which I hoped had not been
smeared with famous poisons.

The dusty heat wrapped round us
like smoke from those volcanoes
we'd seen from the mountain road.
We fished out shillings, packets
of new razor blades. Yet
this was not like other
market scenes where smiles and jokes
help along the bargaining.
These pigmies were humourless

and fiercely eager as if
there were some jungle crisis
to rush back to. What would they
do with this money at the
edge of civilization,
even of their own, for their
tribe lived deep in the forests?

We turned for the mountains
but a smoky black woman
darted forward, thrusting in
frenzy her tiny baby
into the hot space of our
dusty car, into my lap.
She held up a beggar's
cupped hand, but set a price.
Only a shilling for each
rib of the grimy, wrinkled
burden with bones like a bird's
in my hand. I think she
really meant it. The shillings,
the cotton scarf I gave
this mother bird seemed almost
not enough although I was
giving back her offering.
We had no common language,
the pigmy mother and I,
but that frenzy in her eyes,
the passionate thrust away.

I think she really meant it.
I could have bought her baby.

Flamingoes

In the zoo's ornamental water-garden
Ducks and black swans
keep sedate company
With peachy pink flamingoes.
A pretty calendar picture
For Sunday artists.

At Kenya's Lake Nakuru
The painting is boldly splashed,
violently horizontal.
Brown, cracked mud-flats,
Then that focal streak of pink—
Hundreds of thousands of flamingo
Legs beneath the cloud of white.
Across the water, golden larches
And the wide sky.

In the next lake
Flamingoes are dying,
Chained with chalk deposits,
The nurturing water turned hostile.

So I run crazily on to this canvas,
Over the mud-flats.
The cloud sweeps into the air
Dipping red-tipped wings,
And I beg them not to look back,
To remember Lot's wife.

Beethoven

It is inevitable,
the power that will go on
until the world is blown up.
These bold strains
and themes will rise
with the billowing mushroom
from Coventry or Berlin,
Hiroshima, Lebanon
or Cheyenne Mountain hideout.
This is the music the rain
will meet, whatever the tongue
of screams and final silence.
Before those long finales,
heavy climaxes, there will be
underground thumpings of drums,
twitterings of eastern pipes,
voice of the sitar, a moan,
a sigh, and haunting mourning
from mellow Indian flutes.
Then the symphony again
—inevitable—
sound waves that would not flow
in any other way. There was
emptiness. The composer
listened to the darkness and
raised his hand.

The Cemetery In January

Landmarks in this labyrinth
    of woods, hills
and grassy hollows
    are mausolean monuments
like country cottages
    with no view
through coloured glass.
    A green-bronzed stag
forever turns its raised
    and listening head.
Snow covers tracks where
    joggers pounded
over leaves like fluted fans,
    where a child sought
the secret of a boomerang's
    swift orbit.
Under a green and primrose sky
    I brush a stone step
to meditate upon
    the crystal blankness.
A footprint is layered deep
    in glacier green.
The unmarked snow, the boot
    pressing through
to shaped slush, all become
    one
in my suspended vision.
    Wind whips round stones
carving away snow
    in cleft and curve
to leave sculptures of space.
    Breathing out slowly
I am one with the wind.
    It offers me history,
nudges me

to ethereal flight.
In the cemetery I breathe
for all buried there
and wind breathes
for me.
Shivering,
I leave the frozen seat.
At the house is news
of death,
faded yet bright,
yellow paper
of a telegram.